THE PARABLES OF JESUS

Explained Outside the Box

with the Commentary on the Most Important
Phrases of the Gospels

Claudio Patrini

Contents

Introduction

Providing conceptual indications on the meaning of Jesus' parables can help prevent them from being subjected to misleading interpretations.

However, the effectiveness of the parables remains intact even after their conceptual structure has been delineated. Their function, in fact, is to evoke a much more lively and profound understanding than that which can be expressed in concepts.

Commonly the evangelical parables are interpreted on the basis of theological schemes, or are considered as moral exhortations. To express meanings of this type, however, the intellectuals and moralists would have been enough – and their number was already abundant at the time when the parables were exposed.

Anyone who senses the greatness and the exceptional nature of the figure of Jesus can understand that the meaning of his parables must be on a very different level.

Through the parables, we are provided with privileged accesses to reality. Once we have learned to see, we recognize that we are shown a dimension that is not far away, indeed it is always within reach. It can be accessed from anywhere. Even from here.

Parable of the Prodigal Son
(Luk 15, 11-32)

The youngest of two children, he demanded his share of the estate from his father, and left for abroad.

Here he soon squandered his money by living profligately. In addition, a severe famine occurred in that country, and he found himself in extreme poverty. He made some money by grazing pigs, but he was gripped by hunger, to the point that he would have liked to have fed himself with animal food, but not even that was allowed.

He then matured a deep repentance. He realized how ungrateful he had been to his father, and how his loose life had reduced him to a shamefully miserable condition.

He therefore resolved to return home, with the intention of asking his father's forgiveness, and of accepting from him any treatment and any task, even the most modest, in order to get out of the desperate situation in which he found himself.

His father, who saw him arrive when he was still far away, ran to meet him and embraced him; he had sensed his son's feelings, and immediately forgave him. Although the son acknowledged that he was guilty and deserved to be treated like a servant, the father, full of joy, ordered the servants that his son be dressed in the most beautiful suit, that a banquet be prepared for special occasions and that party.

Meanwhile, the other son was working in the fields. On his way home, he heard the music and saw the festivities, and a servant told him what had happened. He felt offended and found his father's behavior unfair, who reserved so many favors for a son who had abandoned him to satisfy his pleasures, while he, who had remained close to him and who had always served him, had never been offered anything such.

The father then went to the eldest son and explained to him that, while he had always been with him, and therefore had always participated in what he possessed, for the younger son it was right to rejoice and celebrate, as that brother of his, from lost had been found, from dead he had returned to life.

***

The son who leaves his father's house is all of us.

The experience of him, who passes for a short period of illusory pleasure and then ends up in desperate suffering, is that of all humanity. It is the experience of leaving the initial condition of unconscious bliss (the earthly paradise), to pass into a condition in which an awareness arises which is however impaired: man in this phase has come out of the protected atmosphere of being, for acquire a new but reductive awareness, which leads him to illusory perceive himself as an individual, endowed with his own thought and will. In this

9

condition, man has lost the connection with being, and this inevitably leads to suffering and despair (the pains suffered by the prodigal son).

The return home of the prodigal son represents the overcoming of the individualistic illusion and the regained dimension of being; but this time it is a fuller dimension, richer in value, because it is no longer unconscious as it was originally.

The other son, who had never moved from his father's house, does not receive the celebrations paid to the prodigal son, because he represents the condition of being unconscious, which does not arouse the joy one feels for the finding of being, after that it had been lost.

It is actually a matter of getting lost and finding oneself, of dying and coming back to life, because only those who know the dimension of being can consider themselves truly alive.

As the parable suggests, a powerful way to return to being is that of humility. When we come to the true and profound awareness of our own nothingness, and abandon all the arrogance on which our "personality" was built - then it is possible that the veil of illusion falls, and that we finally allow reality to reveal itself to us.

Parable of the Good Samaritan
(Luk 10, 25-37)

Jesus was asked how eternal life can be obtained. He answered by pointing out the commandments to love God and neighbor; then urged to clarify who is neighbor, he told the parable of a man who, attacked by some criminals, was robbed, beaten, and finally left to lie on the street.

Both a priest and a man in charge of religious ceremonies passed through that road, but none of them helped the unfortunate.

Then a foreigner passed by. Seeing the conditions of the man who was lying on the road, he felt pity for him. He walked over, washed and bandaged his wounds and transported him to an inn. He stayed by his side for a day and then, having to leave, he made sure he was looked after, at his expense, until his return.

When the story of Jesus was finished, his interlocutor did not hesitate to answer his own question, recognizing that, among the three men who had passed that road, the neighbor was the foreigner who helped the unfortunate.

***

The Samaritan is an example of how one who is free from the self acts. He is not limited by concepts of difference and convenience, he treats others as himself,

11

and does what he feels is necessary for the good of the other.

Only he who abides in being can act in this way, only he who is truly alive. The eternal life preached by Jesus is not something attainable only after the death of the body. It is that dimension out of time, which does not follow, but coincides with loving God and neighbor.

Significantly, Jesus shows that we need to replace the question "who is my neighbor?", with another: "what is the attitude I must have in order to be a neighbor to others?". In other words, instead of turning to evaluate the behavior of others, we must be the ones who realize truth and justice in the world.

The idea that there is a multiplicity of people, and that it is the moral duty of each to act also for the good of others, however, is the result of dualistic thinking, which is flat and dead.

Instead he who, having overwhelmed the illusion of the self, participate in eternal life, is thereby infusing life into the world, creating it: he generates proximity.

Parable of the Talents
(Mat 25, 14-30 ; Luk 19, 12-27)

A man, having to go on a journey, handed over his goods to his servants, giving each according their respective abilities. So to a servant he gave five coins, to another two coins, and to a third servant he gave a coin.

The one who had received five coins used them to earn five more. Even the one who had received two coins, he managed to earn two more with them. Instead, the servant who had received only one coin, did not use it, but dug a hole in the ground and hid it there.

When the master returned, the first two servants showed him, doubled, the money he had entrusted to them. The master praised them for their goodness and their faithfulness and, since they had been faithful in little, gave them power over much, and called them to share in his joy.

The third servant returned to the master only the coin that had been entrusted to him. He justified himself by saying that he was afraid because he knew that his master was a hard man, who expected to reap even where he had not sown.

The master was angry with that servant, whom he described as lazy, wicked and useless, and reproached him for not having taken even a minimal action, such as entrusting the money to a banker, so that he could at least earn interest. He had that servant thrown into the darkness, and he wanted his coin to be given to the one who had ten. "Whoever has increased his wealth will be given further wealth, without limits," he said, "but whoever has not increased his wealth, even what he has will be taken away".

***

The servant who buries the talent received from the master is the one who sticks to his own life, to the idea of being an individual subject.

Own life is the minimum, it is the starting point, it is an illusion that, in itself, leads nowhere.

We need to go further, take at least a few steps towards an increase in reality, otherwise in the end we will lose even what little we have (bare life).

Going beyond could be understood as giving oneself, being generous, but it is not just that. Going beyond rather means exploiting and increasing the wealth of being.

The master "collects where he did not sow": we are beyond the causal logic; in being one gives and receives freely, in abundance, without proportionality. Unlike what happens at the level of the common mentality, in which every fact has a cause proportionate to a previous fact, participating in the being involves a creative process: in every moment something new is born, and in every moment the world itself is recreated.

Parable of the Mustard Seed
(Mat 13, 31-32 ; Mar 4, 30-32 ; Luk 13, 18-19 ; Thomas 20)

The kingdom of heaven can be compared to a mustard seed. It is very small, the smallest of all seeds. But when a man takes it and sows it in his field, it surpasses all the other plants in the garden, and grows to the point of becoming a tree, among whose branches the birds come to make their nests.

***

A fundamental characteristic of life in being (the kingdom of heaven) is that in this dimension the conceptual categories have no meaning.

If we picture God as something greater than anything we can imagine, we are completely off track. In fact, we are still relying on our imagination, on our thinking.

The invitation of this parable, to seek God in what appears small and insignificant, is an attempt to undermine conceptual thought.

It is the overturning of the common mentality. We are used to identifying hierarchical scales in the world, from what is unimportant to what matters most. We consider ourselves, our history and our existence to be very important.

But these hierarchical levels are illusory. The wealth of being spreads without limitations, and all living beings, as well as apparently most irrelevant objects or events, are also a full expression of being.

If the mental constructions that we identify as "people" or "personal stories" are disaggregated, the agitation for what appear to be gains or losses also ceases, and in every moment, in every little part of reality, freedom, joy and love will manifest.

Parable of the Ten Virgins
(Mat 25, 1-13)

Entering the kingdom of heaven is comparable to ten virgins who, taking their lamps, waited to meet the bridegroom. Five virgins were foolish, and five were wise.

While the five foolish virgins took only the lamps with them, the five wise virgins also provided themselves with some supplies of oil.

It got late, and all the virgins eventually fell asleep. Late at night, a cry warned that the bridegroom had arrived, and it was necessary to go immediately to meet him. All the virgins woke up, and realized that the oil contained in the lamps was finished. Then the foolish virgins asked the wise ones for a little of theirs, but they could not give it to them because otherwise the oil would have been insufficient for all of them.

While the foolish virgins went to the vendors to get their supplies of oil, the bridegroom arrived, the wise virgins entered the wedding with him, and the door was closed.

When, later, the foolish virgins also arrived, they insistently begged the bridegroom to let them in. But he denied them entry, and declared that he did not know them.

It is therefore necessary to be vigilant, because it is not given to know either the day or the hour.

***

We must not believe that we can reduce *being* to the size of our mind.

On the surface, the foolish virgins have done nothing wrong, sticking to what is considered normal. But this is precisely the point: as long as one remains in normality, that is, within the context of what is considered reasonable and appropriate, one cannot have access to awakening, to the kingdom of heaven. And in fact when the bridegroom arrives the foolish virgins are deprived of light, and it is impossible for them to meet him. Nor is it possible for wise virgins to give part of their oil to foolish virgins, because the light that allows them to follow the bridegroom cannot be received from outside, or from others.

The spare oil that the wise virgins had is that extra something, something that is beyond what is considered appropriate, reasonable and normal.

We are deceiving ourselves when we imagine the kingdom of heaven as an extension or intensification of the earthly world. It lies beyond the sphere of reason and imagination.

Of course the bridegroom "comes" at any time, and we are usually unprepared and miss meeting him.

Parable of the Sower
(Mat 13,1-23 ; Mar 4,1-20 ; Luk 8,5-15 ; Thomas 9)

The sower went out to sow his seeds. Some seeds fell on the road, and the birds came and ate them. Some seeds fell on stony ground; finding little soil, they sprouted immediately but, having no deep roots, they dried up with the sun. Some seeds fell among the brambles, and these grew and choked them. Some seeds fell on the good soil and gave much fruit.

***

The interior condition necessary to be able to know the truth is described. It is a condition of openness, of tender welcome, of humble expectation. A rigid and excessively involved attitude in external events prevents the truth from making its way into us.

Parable of the Homicidal Tenants
(Mat 21,33-46 ; Mar 12,1-11 ; Luk 20,9-19 ; Thomas 65)

A man planted a vineyard, left it to some farmers, and then left and stayed away for a long time.

When the time came, the owner of the vineyard sent a servant to those peasants to raise his share of the harvest. But the peasants attacked the servant and threw him out.

The master sent another servant, but the peasants beat and insulted this one too, and sent him away.

The third servant that the master sent was also wounded and chased away.

Then the owner of the vineyard thought of sending his own son to those peasants, because at least they would have respect for him.

However, the peasants, believing that if they had killed his son they would have obtained, in his place, the inheritance of the vineyard, they drove him out of the vineyard and killed him.

At this point, what else can the owner of the vineyard do, if not to kill those tenants, and entrust his vineyard to others?

***

We hold fast to the belief that our body is ours, that our life is ours, that our individuality is ours. We consider ourselves to be subjects, and everything we do not perceive as part of us we reject outside, reducing it to an object. We are self-centered, full of conceit, arrogance and ingratitude.

In reality, personal existence is an illusion. Only the One exists, and everything is part of it and is an expression of it. Our existence does not come from us, it is given to us so to speak, and its essence would require it to turn to the being it belongs to, reflecting its freedom and unconditional openness. This would be "to bear the fruits", or to give the owner of the vineyard what is due to him.

The servants that the owner of the vineyard sends to the winemakers are the objects, people and events of life. But we do not recognize them any dignity, and we reject them "outside", considering them as intrusive strangers who try to question our right to be subjects, closed and superior to everything around us.

This attitude reaches the point of wanting to cancel any link with the Whole, that is, with the divinity that is in us. This is how we kill, in ourselves, "the son of the owner of the vineyard", thereby condemning ourselves to ignorance, that is, to remain excluded from life and the light of being.

Parable of the Leaven
(Mat 13,33; Luk 13,20-21 ; Thomas 96)

The kingdom of God can be compared to leaven, which a woman mixes with a large quantity of flour, until it is all leavened.

***

For those who know *being*, the experience of abiding in it can be compared to an expansion. We no longer feel limited to our body and personality, but we feel that everything is part of us (and at the same time we perceive ourselves as part of the whole). One feels animated and supported by a tender and invincible force at the same time, by an inextinguishable ferment of life. St Paul expresses it with these words: "I do not live, but Christ lives in me" (Gal. 2:20).

Parable of the Fig Tree That Sprouts
(Mat 24, 32-36 ; Mar 13,28-32 ; Luk 21, 29-33)

By observing the fig tree and all the trees, you can understand that, when they sprout, summer is near.

Likewise, when you see the upheavals I have described to you, know that the kingdom of God is near. And, in truth, all of this will happen before this generation passes.

***

The appearance of buds on plants testifies to the powerful advance of the seasons, an event that inevitably occurs and over which we have no influence.

Likewise, liberation occurs. It is not something that starts with us; it is something greater than us, in which we are involved without being able to interfere in the slightest.

When liberation occurs, all the bonds and all the apparent certainties that we had fall off. The whole old world is turned upside down, and gives way to a new life.

Parable of the Barren Fig Tree
(Luk 13, 6-9)

A man had planted a fig tree in his field. But when he went to look for fruit, he did not find any, and so it happened for three years in a row.

Since that tree was exploiting the land uselessly, he ordered the farmer to cut it down.

But the farmer suggested that he wait another year. He would have hoed around the tree and put some fertilizer. If, after this intervention, the tree had continued to bear no fruit, then they would have cut it down.

***

Even when it now seems impossible that someone can access true life, he can receive from some circumstance or from some person, with care and completeness, all the conditions for realizing his true nature.

Even if we have been refusing the invitation for a long time, life is always ready to give us everything we need to free us from illusion.

Parable of the Unfaithful Administrator
(Luk 16, 1-8)

A wealthy man was told that his administrator was squandering his possessions. He sent for him, and told him to give an account of his administration, announcing that he would take his job away.

The administrator realized the difficult situation he would find himself in when he was fired. In fact, he did not feel able to carry out strenuous work, nor could he have asked for alms, because he was ashamed.

He then devised a way to find a welcome in someone's home. He spoke to each of his master's debtors. To one who owed a hundred barrels of oil, he commuted the debt to fifty barrels. To another, who owed a hundred measures of grain, he commuted the debt to eighty.

The boss praised the shrewdness of that dishonest administrator. In fact, in dealing with their fellowmen, the children of this world are more cunning than the children of light.

***

Unfaithful administrators are those who have not yet overcome the illusion of being individuals, but who nevertheless strive to do "good" works, with the intent of acquiring the merits to obtain paradise after death.

Since they move within the perspective of the ego, their "good" works are still tainted by selfishness (such as the hope of obtaining heaven for oneself after death); and the means used to benefit others are not proper means (they would be so only if, overcoming the illusion of subjectivity, the "benefactors" canceled themselves to identify with the whole: at that point, every divine prerogative would be theirs too).

However, even good works done to please the ego (subtly), can have positive effects on those who have done them. On the part of those who have been benefited, in fact, a current of gratitude towards the benefactor can originate, and a consonance can be established between them such as to lead to the overcoming of the ego and in communion with the Whole.

Parable of the Workers in the Vineyard
(Mat 20, 1-16)

The kingdom of heaven is comparable to a man who left his house at dawn to hire workers for his vineyard. With those he found, he settled for one denarius a day, and they went into his vineyard and started to work.

About nine in the morning, the master saw other unemployed men in the square, and sent them to work in his vineyard, promising to pay them the fair.

The master went out again about noon, and then about three and about five, and all those who had not found anyone to hire them, he sent them to work in his vineyard.

When evening came, the boss called the workers and ordered them to be paid, starting with those who arrived last, up to the first.

Those who arrived at five each received a denarius. Seeing this, those who arrived first expected to be paid more, but they also received a denarius. They complained then to the master, that they were treated in the same way as those who had worked much less than them.

The master replied that he was not doing them any wrong, because he was giving them exactly the compensation he had promised. And if he wanted to give the same compensation to the newcomers as well, this was within his full right to dispose of his possessions as he pleased. On the contrary, he asked those who were complaining if the reason for their recrimination was not envy for his goodness. So the last will be the first, and the first, the last.

***

We all, sooner or later, are called to work in the vineyard. We work in the vineyard of the One when our life becomes tiring, and we have to take hard blows and suffer heavy losses.

Someone is called to suffer more than others, but in the end the expected result (the compensation at the end of the working day) is the same for everyone: liberation from illusion.

In the field of being, there is no earthly accounting: there is no greater reward for those who have worked more. It is the kingdom of freedom: no borders are drawn here, but every good is bestowed without limits and distinctions. The last and the first, in this realm, are interchangeable and are confused with each other.

Parable of the Two Sons
(Mat 21, 28-31)

A man, who had two sons, asked the first to go to work in the vineyard. The son replied that he did not want to; but then, repenting, he went there.

The man also asked the same thing to the second son. That son replied with deference that he would go there; but then he didn't go there.

Jesus asked: - Which of the two sons did the father's will?

- They answered: the first.

- Well, I tell you the truth: in the kingdom of God, tax collectors and prostitutes precede you.

***

The son who declares his refusal to follow his father's will, but who then carries it out, represents those who clearly see the alternative between following his own ego and abandoning it. They are aware of not being able to abandon the illusion of subjectivity; however, at the basis of their initial choice there is a base of honesty and clarity, and on this basis it will also be possible for them to overcome the illusion of the ego.

The son who claims that he wants to follow his father's will, but then does not carry it out, represents those who are trapped in the swamp of thought. They think mentally that they share their father's will and that they have freed themselves from their own subjective will. But it is only an intellectual conviction, which has nothing to do with reality. They have not achieved the overcoming of subjectivity at all, they have only thought about it. But the very belief that they have already reached the goal is what precludes them from an effective realization.

Parable of the Lost Sheep
(Mat 18, 12-14 ; Luk 15, 4-7 ; Thomas 107)

Who, having a hundred sheep, lost one, would not leave the other ninety-nine, and would not stop looking for the lost one until he found it?

Once he found it, he would load it onto his shoulders and return home full of joy, and call friends and neighbors to rejoice with him.

Likewise, there will be more joy in heaven for a sinner who is converted than for ninety-nine righteous who have never gone astray.

***

The shepherd who leaves the other sheep to dedicate himself to finding the lost sheep represents the immeasurable love of God for all men. The shepherd's action conveys the idea of how all forces are channeled towards that one man who must be helped to find *being*. The entire universe works for the salvation of a single man.

Everything is One: therefore not even a single element can be left out of the harmony of truth.

Parable of the Lost Coin
(Luk 15, 8-10)

If a woman who has ten coins loses one, doesn't she light the lamp and sweep the whole house and keep searching carefully until she finds it? Then she calls her friends and neighbors to rejoice with her for having found the coin she had lost.

Likewise there is joy among the angels of God, for a single sinner who is converted.

***

As in the parable of the lost sheep, here too it is shown how precious the event of conversion is.

When someone who was "lost" is found, it is as if the entire universe exulted, regenerated.

It can be said that when even a single person accesses the truth, it is the whole world that accesses truth and salvation.

Parable of the Lamp
(Mat 5, 14-16 ; Mar 4, 21-23 ; Luk 8, 16-18)

You are the light of the world.

A city on top of a mountain cannot remain hidden. A lamp is not lit to be placed in a hidden corner, but rather to be placed on the candelabra, so that it spreads its light throughout the house.

***

Every man is a source of light, a very pure source of freedom. Men themselves are not aware of it, so their greatness seems to remain hidden, secret. But in reality nothing is hidden, their light shines magnificently, and their greatness is comparable to the majesty of a village located on top of a hill. Man believes he has to fight with the world to snatch its advantages, while in reality he is its lord and soul.

Man is not simply an element of the world, alongside other elements. He is not a "subject" beyond which an "external" world extends. There is no subject, no external world, only being. Insofar as he lives and participates in being, man creates himself and the world in every instant.

33

Parable of the Darnel
(Mat 13, 24-30; Thomas 57)

The kingdom of heaven is like a man who sows good grain in his field. But his enemy, when everyone was asleep, came and, in the midst of the wheat, sowed darnel.

As the wheat grew, so did the darnel. The peasants reported it to the owner of the field, and asked him to uproot it.

But the master knew that this was the work of his enemy. He did not want the peasants to uproot the darnel, to prevent the wheat from being damaged by doing so.

He arranged for the time to be expected when the grain would be ripe. Then the peasants would have collected the darnel first, to burn it. Then they could collect the grain and put it back in its granaries.

***

Every man has within him the good seeds and the seeds of the darnel.

When man reaches the maturity to which he is called, he realizes his true nature; and in doing this all illusory conceptions (the darnel) automatically dissolve and are separated from him.

Parable of the Merciless Servant
(Mat 18, 23-35)

The kingdom of heaven is like a king who decided to settle the unfinished business with his servants. Since one of these was indebted to him for ten thousand talents, the master ordered that he be sold with his entire family and all his possessions, in order to repay the debt. That servant then prostrated himself to the ground and begged him to be patient, because he would give him back everything he owed him. The master, taking pity, forgave him the debt.

Shortly thereafter, that same servant met a companion of his who owed him a hundred denarii. He violently attacked him, demanding that he pay him back the debt. The man prostrated himself to the ground and begged him to be patient, but he didn't want to know, and had him put in prison until he had paid all his due.

The other servants, disapproving of this behavior, reported to the master what had happened.

The master, having him summoned, reproached that man for his wickedness, and handed him over to the torturers to pay back all his debt.

This is how Heavenly Father will behave, with all those who do not sincerely forgive their brothers.

***

We are all guilty, we all owe a huge debt to God.

If we believe we are individuals and identify with our body and mind, it means that we are not living in union with God, we are not responding to the heartfelt and continuous appeal that his infinite love sends us: we are not giving him back the immense gifts that are offered to us, and therefore we are indebted to him and need his forgiveness.

Since we are all at fault and in debt with respect to what is of utmost importance, and indeed is uniquely important and real, it is unjustified and reprehensible that we do not forgive those who owe us in matters whose importance is irrelevant to the plane of truth and being.

For those who participate in being, an attitude of unlimited compassion and forgiveness towards his fellow men is spontaneous.

The inability to forgive indicates that we are still prisoners of the illusion of individuality. Lacking union with being, those who find themselves in this condition will perceive a continuous state of deprivation, and therefore will not be able to avoid suffering.

Parable of the Pharisee and the Tax Collector
(Luk 18, 9-14)

A Pharisee and a tax collector went to the temple to pray.

The Pharisee considered himself a righteous man, in fact he fasted twice a week and paid tithes on all his possessions. Standing upright, he thanked God for not being, like other men, guilty of injustice, theft, adultery. And he too thanked him for not being like that tax collector who was also in the temple.

The tax collector, on the other hand, had stopped on the sidelines. He dared not look up, and he beat his chest begging God to have mercy on him, who knew he was a sinner.

Now, unlike the Pharisee, the tax collector returned home justified. For whoever humbles himself will be exalted, and whoever exalts himself will be humbled.

***

External actions, however altruistic they may seem, have no importance except in relation to the motivation that inspires them.

The Pharisee, with his seemingly flawless actions, is only feeding his own ego. He is not arrogant only in the common sense of the term, but he is also arrogant in a deeper sense, because he is convinced that he is an individual and that he is acting for the best; therefore he has developed a more subtle but no less solid and harmful self-consciousness.

The tax collector is not (yet) what God wants him to be, but he has triggered a fundamental process: he questions his own self, feels its insufficiency and baseness, perceives his own littleness and feels the need to cancel himself in relation to what is immensely larger. He is in the phase in which man ends, and the divine begins.

Parable of Lazarus and the Rich Epulon
(Luk 16,19-31)

There was a rich man, named Epulon, who wore refined clothes and who indulged in sumptuous lunches every day. At his door stood a poor man, named Lazarus, who hoped to feed himself with the scraps of the rich man's banquets. Nobody cared about him, except the dogs that came to lick his sores.

One day Lazarus died, and the angels took him to heaven, next to Abraham. Epulon also died, and ended up in the flames of hell. Seeing Lazarus and Abraham in the distance, he invoked Abraham to send Lazarus to refresh him, with a few drops of water, from the heat that tortured him.

Abraham, however, declared that it was not possible to change his condition, nor that of Lazarus: whoever had received his goods in life, now necessarily had to receive the torments; and who in life had received pains, now received consolations.

Then Epulon begged Abraham to at least send Lazarus to his family to admonish his five brothers not to repeat his mistakes, so as to save themselves from the pains of hell. Abraham replied that the words of Moses and the Prophets were already there to indicate the path to follow. Epulon answered back that seeing someone who presented himself from the realm of the dead, his brothers would be converted. But Abraham said that if they did not listen to Moses and the Prophets, they would not be convinced even by seeing someone rise from the dead.

***

The more one seeks satisfaction in material goods, the more one precludes oneself from the infinitely superior satisfaction of abiding in one's true nature. Pursuing material gratifications is one way (and it is not the only one) to cultivate one's ego and please it, while remaining insensitive towards one's fellow men.

Finding one's true nature implies a total extraneousness to the attraction for material satisfactions, in the sense that one does not seek one's happiness in them.

The teachings transmitted in the sacred texts of every religion are often the testimony of men who have overcome illusion, and who have participated in the truth of being. Theirs are powerful words, capable of inducing conversion. Those who, from contact with these teachings, do not feel the impulse for a transformation, much less could receive help from witnessing "miraculous" events.

However, it must be clear that the events of life and those, apparently consequent, of heaven and hell, should not be understood on two separate temporal planes.

They coexist. Talking about a before (life) and an after (heaven and hell) only makes sense if you are addressing those who have not yet abandoned the dualistic consciousness: in the dimension of being, the illusion of time disappears.

Parable of the First Places and of the Invitations
(Luk 14, 7-11)

When you are invited to a wedding banquet, do not put yourself first, because you may be forced to give that place to someone more worthy than you, and then you will be ashamed of having to put yourself to the bottom.

When you are invited to a wedding, put yourself in the last place instead; so it may happen that the one who invited you asks you, as a sign of friendship, to move forward, thus giving you honor in front of all the diners.

Because whoever exalts himself will be humbled, and whoever humbles himself will be exalted.

***

If we are victims of the ego's deception, we tend to place ourselves above everything and everyone and move away from truth and being; so in reality our value plummets to very low levels.

Instead, the more we are free from the illusion of the ego and the more we feel small, the closer we are to being, and we participate in its immense value.

42

Parable of the Wedding Banquet
(Mat 22, 1-14 ; Luk 14, 16-24 ; Thomas 64)

A man organized a large dinner, and sent out many invitations. But when he sent his servant to call the guests, they all made an excuse and refused to come. Someone because he had to go and see some land he had just bought; someone because he had to check some newly bought oxen; someone because he had just got married and therefore couldn't come.

When the servant told him that everyone had refused the invitation, the master was angry, and ordered the servant to go out into the streets and squares and to bring to his dinner all the poor and invalids that he would find.

Since there was still room, the master ordered the servant to go out again and bring to his house all those he could find even in the ravines and along the hedges: in fact, none of those who had initially been invited, would have tasted his dinner.

***

Whoever does not recognize the illusiveness of the world as it is commonly perceived, and is completely involved in it and in the deceptive values that the mind constructs, cannot accept the call of being.

43

Instead he resides in being, and discovers his true nature, the one who lives in a condition of "spiritual beggar". He is "homeless" because he is devoid of ties to earthly goods and values.

In reality, the invitation of being is so pressing and thoughtful that no one is excluded. And it is more likely to best reach those who, in the eyes of the world, occupy the lowest and most disadvantaged positions.

Parable of the Good Shepherd
(Joh 10, 1-16)

While the shepherd enters the sheep pen from the door, whoever enters it from the other side is a thief or a criminal.

The shepherd calls each of his sheep by name.

He walks ahead of them, and they follow him, because they recognize his voice. On the other hand, they will not follow a stranger, because they will not recognize his voice.

***

The truth is always direct, open. It does not follow cross roads and ambiguous paths.

The voice of truth is intimately recognized. It creates a deep resonance within us, it is familiar and close to us. Closer than we are to ourselves.

Parable of the Seed That Sprouts by Itself
(Mar 4, 26-29)

The kingdom of God is like a man who puts a seed in the ground. Without himself knowing how, and whether he sleeps or watches, night or day, the seed sprouts and grows. From the ground the stem is produced first, and then the ear, which finally becomes full of grains. Then when the ear is ripe, man has it mowed because it is harvest time.

***

The way in which awareness of our true nature grows in us is mysterious. It is a maturation that follows its own laws, regardless of what we do or don't do. When the journey is completed, the fruit is picked and the transformation is definitive.

Parable of the Hidden Treasure

Parable of the Pearl
(Mat 13, 44-46 ; Thomas 109 ; 76)

The kingdom of heaven is like a treasure hidden in a field. A man finds it. He first of all hides it with care; then, filled with joy, he goes to sell all his possessions and with the proceeds he buys that field.

The kingdom of heaven is also like a merchant who is dedicated to the search for gemstones. Once he finds a gemstone of great value, he immediately goes to sell all of his possessions, and buys that gemstone.

***

Anyone who recognizes the value of reality that lies beyond the illusion of the senses and the ego, knows that nothing can be compared to it. Along with joy of having awakened from the dream, he feels detached from all that is considered precious in the eyes of the world.

Clearly, the values of the world and the values of being are incompatible, and mutually exclusive. There are no middle ways or partial pursuits: choosing being implies that you accept it in its entirety, and that you completely free yourself from the illusory perception of the world.

Parable of the Scribe Disciple of the Kingdom of Heaven
(Mat 13, 51-52)

Every student of the scriptures, when he becomes a disciple of the kingdom of heaven, is like a householder who examines his treasure, and extracts new things and old things from it.

***

The texts of the wisdom traditions are a living source of truth. There are no fixed and immutable concepts or dogmas in them. The truths indicated in them are such to the extent that they are revitalized each time by those who know how to interpret them by reliving them in themselves. They are therefore both perennial and always new. Not belonging to the sphere of conceptual thought, eternal truths are clear and unambiguous, and yet they are also multifaceted and elusive.

Parable of the Net
(Mat 13, 47-50 ; Thomas 8)

The kingdom of heaven is like a net thrown into the sea. It collects fish of all kinds and, once it is full, the fishermen pull it ashore and carefully examine its contents. They separate the good fish, which they collect in the baskets, from the bad fish, which they throw away.

The same will happen at the end of the world. The angels will come to separate the good men from the bad ones, and the latter will be thrown into the fiery furnace, where their suffering will be great.

***

Life is not to be wasted. If in our existence we have not come to know our true nature and therefore our identity with being, everything we have experienced will remain worthless, because it is confined to the realm of illusion. Only by coming to recognize the truth do we come to find ourselves in the field of what has value, because it is real.

Parable of the Salt of the Earth
(Mat 5,13 ; Mar 9,50)

You are the salt of the earth. But if the salt lacks its flavor, what will make it salty? It will do no good, and it will be thrown away and trampled underfoot.

***

Man is called to detach himself from the kingdom of nature; he cannot limit himself to being part of the dead and deterministic environment that seems to surround him.

By discovering his true nature, man becomes a source of freedom, a bearer of meaning. He can illuminate and enliven what surrounds him.

If he does not rise above himself, that is, above being a simple component of nature, man remains worthless.

Parable of the Sheep and Goats
(Mat 25, 31-46)

When the Son of man will manifest himself in his glory, he will sit on the throne, and all the angels will be with him. All peoples will gather before him, and he will separate one from another, as a shepherd separates the sheep from the goats.

He will put the sheep on his right hand, and the goats on his left. He will welcome as blessed by the Heavenly Father those who are on his right, and he will offer them as an inheritance the kingdom prepared for them since the creation of the world, for they had given him to eat when he was hungry, they had given him to drink when he was thirsty, they had dressed him when he was naked, they had looked after him when he was sick, they had welcomed him when he was a foreigner and they had gone to visit him when he was in prison.

The righteous will then ask him when they did all this for him, and the Lord will answer them that everything they did to only one of his little ones brothers, they did to him.

Then turning to those on his left, he will call them cursed and drive them away from him, towards the eternal fire prepared for the devil, for they did not give him food when he was hungry, they did not give him drink when he was thirsty, they had not dressed him when he was naked, they had not assisted him when he was ill, they had not welcomed him when he was a foreigner and they had not gone to visit him when he was in prison.

They will ask him when they have failed to do all this for him, and he will answer them that everything they did not do to one of his little ones brothers, they did not do to him.

***

Whoever does not submit to discriminating thought and dualistic illusion, recognizes the One in everything and in every person, and is animated, towards everything and every person, by a fraternal spirit. Such a person currently dwells in being, in "eternal life".

Parable of the Foolish Rich Man
(Luk 12, 16-21)

A rich man had had a bountiful harvest on his land. He then began to think about where to store that crop, because his warehouses would not be sufficient to contain it.

He decided that he would demolish his warehouses and build larger ones, where he could store all his grain and his possessions.

Once this was done, he thought, he would have enough possessions at his disposal for many years, and he could rest, spend his life eating, drinking and entertaining.

But God reproached him for his foolishness: for that same night life would be required of him, and all his preparations to whom would they benefit?

This happens to those who accumulate wealth for themselves, without getting rich with God.

***

Anything based on the ego's perspective is illusory. Whatever the thoughts, achievements and power that the ego seems to deploy, these are always appearances, which can dissolve at any moment.

Men tend to believe that they can base their lives on a sure foundation; but the possession of material goods, the power over others, their very identity have nothing solid, they are only mental constructions.

What really has value is being, which is accessed through the recognition that the I, and all its constructions, are a deception.

The rich man, of whom the parable speaks, is not simply the one who has accumulated many riches according to the common criteria of value. Anyone who thinks he has a body, an independent will, his own morality is rich; anyone who believes he has rights (or duties) and merits (or faults) is rich; anyone who believes he has a personal story and the time available to organize his life is rich.

Ultimately, anyone who thinks he possesses an individuality is rich, and is bound by it.

Parable of the Importunate Friend
(Luk 11, 5-13)

If someone, having nothing to offer a friend who has come from a long journey, knocks on a friend's door at midnight to ask him to borrow bread, he may hear from his friend that it is too late, because the whole family is already in bed and it is not possible for him to get up.

However, if he insists on the request, that friend, if not out of friendship at least to stop the annoyance, will get up and give him the requested bread.

In fact, if you ask, you will receive, if you search, you will find, if you knock, it will be opened to you.

No father would give a snake to a son who asks for a fish, nor would he give him a scorpion if the son asks for an egg. Therefore, if men, who are evil, give good things to their children, much more the Father of Heaven will give, to those who ask him, the Spirit.

***

The truth of being is open and accessible to all, but it is necessary to "ask ... seek ... knock ...": that is, it is necessary to get out of the usual ways of thinking, and have a yearning beyond them, looking in directions that are normally neglected.

Whoever seeks finds, whoever asks receives, whoever knocks will be opened: in fact, the truth of being is not hidden, and access to it is not subject to any constraints.

Constantly, and with the utmost strength, the being calls us to welcome and embrace us. It is we who place a barrier and, by closing ourselves in the self, we prevent entry to the truth.

A glimmer is enough, a minimum willingness to get out of the mental schemes and, while we are even just hinting at "knocking", we will realize that the door to truth is already opening wide. Indeed, we will realize that it had never been closed.

Parable of the Master and the Servant
(Luk 17, 7-10)

When the servant returns from the field after plowing, or after grazing the flock, no master will tell him to come and sit at the table. Each master will rather tell him to prepare food and to serve it, and only after the master has eaten and drunk will he give the servant permission to eat and drink in turn.

And no master will feel gratitude for that servant, because he has only carried out the orders received.

Likewise everyone, after having done what he has been ordered, will have to believe that he is only a useless servant, who has done what he had to do.

***

Only if the ego is completely annihilated, the conditions are created for one's divine nature to emerge. As long as there is even a minimum feeling of having value, of having merits and rights, you will not be able to have access to being.

It is not about compressing one's free will. It is about recognizing that *there is no* free will. What happens happens, in total freedom of being: no one has "wanted" it.

The attitude of the useless servant described in the parable is only apparently limiting. In fact, the individual will is only an illusion; when you stop believing in it, you find yourself sharing the boundless freedom of being.

Parable of the Unjust Judge
(Luk 18, 1-8)

In one city there was a judge who had no fear of God or respect for men. A widow persistently went to this judge to ask for justice against her opponent.

Despite having no regard for that widow, the judge decided to do her justice, in order to no longer be bothered by her requests.

So if even that dishonest judge finally accepted the requests that were made to him, will not God be infinitely more solicitous in granting justice to his elect? He will certainly not make them wait long, but rather he will do them justice promptly.

But at the coming of the Son of man, there will be faith on earth?

***

We must seek truth and justice relentlessly, without losing heart and without doubting that we can reach them. If this strong and sincere longing animates us, truth and justice will come to us much sooner than we expect.

God's justice, however, is not that of this world. Finding justice means being free from the constructions and attachments of the mind. Then it will be discovered that everything is an expression of God, everything is right and perfect.

We will find justice in us, and therefore throughout the world.

This attitude is "faith", that is, the prerequisite for the coming of the Son of man.

Parable of the Grain of Wheat
(Joh 12,24-25)

If the grain of wheat, placed in the ground, does not die, it remains alone; if it dies, it produces much fruit.

Whoever loves his life, loses it, and whoever hates his life in this world, will keep it in eternal life.

***

As long as one remains tied to the illusory identification with a body and with certain psychological characteristics, knowledge of one's true nature is precluded.

To the extent that one's apparent individual identity is abandoned, one opens up to an infinitely vaster and truer reality.

We then discover that we are not, as was previously believed, something single and limited. With any object or person we come in contact with, we rightfully feel that that thing or person is part of us, it is ourselves. And, likewise, we recognize that we are in turn part of the whole.

In the expression "to hate one's life", the verb "to hate" must be understood mainly as "to detach oneself, to distance oneself". Also wanting to give a more literal meaning to the aforementioned expression, it must be understood as getting bored and detesting the anguish and pettiness of one's particularities, one's silly attachments, one's narrow selfishness.

Parable of the Vine and the Branches
(Joh 15, 1-8)

I am the real vine, and the Father is the farmer. He cuts every branch that bears no fruit, and prunes every branch that bears fruit, so that it bears more fruit.

Thanks to the truth that I have announced to you, you are already pure. Stay in me, and I in you. I am the vine, you are the branches. To bear fruit, you must stay in me, as the branch cannot bear fruit by itself, but must stay in the vine.

Without me you can do nothing. Whoever does not stay in me is discarded like the branch, which then dries up and is burned.

If you stay in me and my words in you, you can ask for anything, and it will be done for you.

In this the Father is glorified: that you become my disciples and bear much fruit.

***

If you live connected to being, you are vital and are able to bring forth new gifts for life. If, on the other hand, one does not get out of the illusion of individualism, one remains separated from life, worthless and useless.

It is conceptual, static and dualistic thinking that keeps us in the illusion of an individual, separate existence. But real life is only in being, in the One.

Parable of the Faithful Servant
(Mat 24, 42-51 ; Mar 13, 33-37 ; Luk 12, 35-48)

Be ready! Do as those servants who await the return of the master from the wedding, dressed and with the lamps lit, so that, when the master arrives and knocks, they open for him immediately. Blessed are those servants if, arriving in the middle of the night or before dawn, the master finds them awake, because he himself will serve them.

If the landlord knew the time of the thief's coming, he would not be robbed. So you too are ready, because the Son of man will come when you do not imagine it.

Blessed is that trusted and prudent administrator who, in the absence of the master, manages the servants following the orders received from the master. If on his return the master finds him doing this, he will entrust him with the management of all his possessions. If, on the other hand, counting on the fact that the master's return seems to be delayed, he begins to mistreat the servants, guzzling and getting drunk, he will be severely punished when, in a day and an hour that he does not expect, the master return.

The servant who, knowing the master's will, will not conform to it, will be severely punished. On the other hand, that servant who, not knowing it, will have performed actions worthy of punishment, will be punished less heavily. For whoever was given much, much will be asked.

***

The attitude of listening to the truth only in certain circumstances, which are more comfortable and normal for us, does not work. The necessary attitude is that of constant and total openness, without reservations and without pauses. There must be an absolute yearning for the truth. Then in an unpredictable moment, the recognition of being can happen. It is a relationship with something much greater than us; but at the same time we discover that it is a greatness that invades us from within, comes from us and has always been our true nature.

One cannot relate to the eternal with the ways and times of the common mentality. The eternal sweeps away these ways, it is in antithesis with them. As long as we imagine that to meet the eternal "we have time", or that we have to prepare ourselves and therefore "we need time", we remain in the mentality that precludes that encounter. There is no time, because the eternal is out of time.

Parable of the Two Debtors
(Luk 7, 41-43)

A man boasted a credit from two debtors. The debt of one debtor was five hundred denarii, while the debt of the other was fifty denarii. Neither of them could pay him back, so he forgave both of them.

Which of the two debtors will have greater love for the creditor?

Someone replied that he assumed he was the one who had been forgiven the greatest debt, and Jesus approved of his answer.

***

Whoever recognizes the pettiness of his own ego, knows that he has stained himself with many faults and that he is unworthy of being loved. Yet, he notes, life is still granted to him, a sign that despite all, love has not been denied him. He then feels that he has nothing to demand and everything to give, in order to repay the wrongs committed; and he thus reaches a profound level of humility and unconditional generosity.

Ultimately, whoever denies himself multiplies the love he gives and the love he receives.

The causal relationship between loving and being forgiven goes both ways, because time does not actually exist: seeing events in succession is the result of illusory mental activity.

Parable of New Wine in Old Wineskins
(Mat 9, 16-17 ; Mar 2, 21-22 ; Luk 5, 36-39 ; Thomas 47)

Nobody puts a piece of raw cloth on an old dress, because the patch would take something off the dress and the tear would become worse.

Nor is new wine poured into old wineskins, because the skins would crack and the wine would be lost.

Instead, by pouring new wine into new wineskins, both are preserved.

***

The truth of being, which is "new" and different from the conceptual elaborations, cannot be reconciled with the modalities of the reasoning mind.

The message of non-duality cannot be accepted in the old conceptual schemes: a predisposition of another nature is needed.

The reality of being (which is non-dual) belongs to a different dimension from that which can be represented through thought. Interactions between the "old" (the deceptive representation of the world generated by the mind) and the "new" (the being, the One) are not possible: either you are on one side or the other. It is

70

illusory to believe that one can reach the "new" starting from the "old" and moving within it.

Access to being involves a rebirth, and transforms into new men. At the same time, only new men, who are born to true life, can welcome the truth of being.

Parable of the Unfinished Tower
(Luk 14,25-33)

Whoever does not love me more than he loves his father, mother, wife, children, brothers and even his own life, cannot be my disciple.

Whoever wants to build a tower will first carefully calculate the cost, to understand if he will be able to complete it. In fact, if he were to leave the building halfway through, he would be laughed at by everyone.

Similarly, a king, before waging war on another king, will calculate if he has an army sufficient to defeat him; if not, he will rather send messengers to ask for peace.

Thus, whoever does not renounce all that he possesses cannot be my disciple.

***

To truly follow the teaching of Jesus, it is not enough to accept some aspects of it, and to continue with one's life for the rest. You cannot follow Jesus only in part: either you follow him totally, or you completely miss his message.

What is at stake is a radical choice. Only if you are totally devoid of any connection with the world can you access the deepest reality - in which you will find, multiplied to infinity, that love that, before, was suffocated and obscured by perceiving yourself as separate individuals.

The requirement for liberation is not to simply give up your *possessions*: it is to give up everything you *have*. When we are subjected to the illusion of being separate individuals, everything that is perceived outside of us (even loved ones) is seen in relation to us, and with it we establish bonds and develop attachment. More or less consciously and subtly, we feel we are increasing and strengthening our own selves by strengthening those bonds. This is what Jesus means by "possessing". By asking us to detach ourselves from this, Jesus invites us to abandon what is inherent with possession: the illusion of the self.

Parable of the Bridegroom's Friends
(Mat 9,15 ; Mar 2, 19-20 ; Luk 5, 33-35)

It was objected to Jesus that John's disciples, as well as the disciples of the Pharisees, fasted and prayed often; his disciples, on the other hand, ate and drank.

Jesus replied that bridegroom' friends cannot fast when the bridegroom is with them. But the days would come when the bridegroom would no longer be with them, and then they would fast.

***

For those who already reside in the truth, it makes no sense to practice restrictions and ascetic disciplines, because there is no goal to be achieved in the future, through them.

There may then be circumstances in life for which practicing deprivation is appropriate: life itself will indicate this.

Parable of the Divided Kingdom

Parable of the Strong Man
(Mat 12, 24-30 ; Mar 3, 22-27 ; Luk 11, 14-22)

To the Pharisees, who accused him of casting out demons through Beelzebul, the leader of the demons, Jesus replied: "No kingdom, city or family can stand if it is divided within itself. If Satan casts out Satan, he is divided in himself, so how will his kingdom stand?

So if I do not cast out demons through Beelzebul, but through the Spirit of God, then the kingdom of God has come among you".

No one can enter the house of a strong man and rob his possessions, unless he first binds that strong man.

Whoever is not with me, he is against me, and whoever does not gather with me, scatters".

***

To settle in the realm of good (truth), one must have completely taken over evil (illusion, ignorance). There can be no intermediate situation.

Only those who know they have defeated evil have the certainty of residing in good. If the fight against evil has not been won (or even undertaken), surely the goal of good has not been achieved.

Only if you walk on the ground of reality, you participate in the creativity of life and build good things.

If you do not follow this path, you necessarily go in the opposite direction, that of illusion, in which reality is not touched and nothing good is created.

Parable of the Children in the Square
(Mat 11, 16-17 ; Luk 7, 31-32)

The people of this generation are similar to children who, in the square, shout at each other: "We played the flute and you didn't dance, we sang a lament and you didn't cry!"

***

He who is sincerely and totally open, perceives in every object and in every circumstance the heartfelt voice of being, which calls him to participate in life.

For those who do not have this openness, the messages of being remain unheard, because they are unable to overcome the insensitive armor of the ego.

External circumstances are also invitations, stimuli to develop the right response.

It is necessary to be like good musical instruments, which resound docilely and faithfully to the skilled touches of the player.

Parable of the House Built on the Rock
(Mat 7, 24-27 ; Luk 6, 46-49)

Whoever hears my words, and carries them out, is like a wise man who has founded his house on rock. The rain came, the rivers overflowed and the winds hit that house, and it did not fall.

But whoever hears my words but does not carry them out is like a foolish man who founded his house on the sand. The rain came, the rivers overflowed and the winds hit that house, and it fell, with great ruin.

***

Understanding the truth taught by Jesus means incarnating it, concretely transforming one's being and one's perception of the world.

Whoever appropriates the teaching of Jesus only on a conceptual or sentimental level, has completely missed it; it will have no effect on him and will not subtract him from that ephemeral existence to which almost all people remain tied.

Implementing the truth means accessing reality, and building on the solid ground of being. The teaching has been put into practice if we come to recognize that we are part of God, and that we are God.

Those who are rooted in being can no longer be overwhelmed by the adversities of life, as happens instead for those who believe they can only found themselves on the level of appearance. Adversity continues to occur as always, but their violence no longer has a conditioning effect on those who reside in being.

Parable of the Empty Jar
(Thomas 97)

The Father's Kingdom is like a woman who went a long way carrying a jar full of flour.

Without her noticing and being able to regret it, the handle of the jar broke, and the flour spilled on the road behind her.

When she got home and put down the pitcher, she found it empty.

***

The jar that progressively loses all its content and remains empty, represents the person who frees himself of all the contents of subjectivity, of all judgments and attachments, to finally find himself available to welcome the universality of being.

Parable of the Murderer
(Thomas 98)

The Father's Kingdom is like a man who wanted to kill an important person.

To find out if his hand would be steady, he drew his sword in his house and pierced the wall.

Then he killed the important person.

***

To access the realm of being, it is necessary to know how to go beyond the limits of what is considered normal.

The canons of dualistic thinking are the walls of the prison that preclude us from the perception of being. If you don't question the commonly accepted way of seeing the world, you will never get out of your prison.

To break the illusion of subjectivity, it is necessary to "pierce the wall". It is a swerve, a step that seems enormous and impossible in the eyes of those who cannot get out of the dualistic mind. But nothing less than this will be enough.

Commentary on some Words of Jesus

Whoever wants to follow me, take up his cross and follow me

Normally we spend our entire life trying to reach the most favorable conditions, and to avoid or reduce the impact of the unfavorable ones.

The way indicated by Jesus is instead that of not concentrating one's efforts on the (vain) objective of avoiding suffering. Starting from the acceptance of the specific suffering of one's life, the condition will spontaneously be created to access being, that dimension that generates and includes, without being altered, the particularities of an individual life.

I did not come to bring peace, but the sword

Opening up to reality destroys all ideas, beliefs and the common way of seeing the world. The habitual worldview is upset, annulled. The person with whom we identified ourselves is also erased. All the certainties of thought and of the senses evaporate, and with them also the conviction, which we have always nurtured, of existing as individuals.

The world, as we commonly represent it, is not "pacified" and stabilized when the truth is manifested: on the contrary, it is opposed and totally revolutionized.

Whoever invites to awaken do not indulge men in their reclining in a dream world created by the mind, and rather cause the upheaval and destruction of the dream.

Whoever loves father, mother, children more than me, is not worthy of me

Until we have freed ourselves from illusion, even those that are considered the most sincere feelings are only the shadow of true love, because they are inevitably conditioned by the underlying belief, proper to every human being, of existing as individual subjects.

It is a subtle but decisive egoism, which alters and degrades both understanding and the emotional sphere.

In the moment in which, opening up to being, the bonds and affections developed in the context of individualistic awareness are overcome, one discovers that true love is limitless, has an unimaginable strength, and is not comparable with the feeling that commonly goes by that name.

Whoever finds his life will lose it, and whoever loses his life because of me will find it

Whoever wants to come after me denies himself

There are no loopholes: to find *being*, you have to completely lose yourself.

Even the thinnest thread that connects us to what we think is our individual identity is a chain that denies us liberation.

Every compromise, every half measure, every propensity for a gradual path are only the testimony that we are still separated from the realm of freedom.

There is no real difference between a "selfish and mean" self, and a "higher, more mature, purer" self: as long as the self dominates the conscience, there can be no room for God.

Those who spend their existence without waking up from the dream of the ego live an apparent life, and not the real life.

The Son of man has nowhere to lay his head

Those who dwell in being are totally devoid of the stable references and certainties that conceptual thinking seems to provide.

From the common point of view, this appears to be a vulnerable and insecure life.

From the point of view of being, this is freedom.

The last will be the first, and the first the last

It may help to conceive the "logic" of the world of being as completely overturned with respect to that of common thought.

While in the common mentality the value is made to reside in what is great, powerful and dominant, in the world of being the value resides in what is minimal, humble, and which does not prevail but leaves room for the other.

Every time you understand how to overturn the normal way of seeing the world, you get a taste of being, a taste of the fundamental reality.

Render to Caesar what belongs to Caesar, and to God what belongs to God

The world of the senses and conceptual thinking is totally different from the world of being. The dualism that characterizes the common representation of the world cannot describe or imagine the One.

Therefore it is important not to confuse the two planes, that of illusion and that of reality. We must strive to always adhere to the real world, being careful not to get entangled in the world of appearances.

There is no point in clinging to what is of value only for dealing with practical matters (such as money). On the other hand, it is fundamental to recognize the importance of what constitutes the ultimate nature of the world and of life itself.

Just as money comes from earthly authorities, and in that narrow area it remains, so our true nature comes from being, and it is our task to turn our life to being.

Only those who know they have nothing - not even those characteristics that usually make us believe we are individuals, different and separate from everything else - can be truly poor.

Blessed are the afflicted, for they will be comforted

Sorrow is a powerful way to break away from illusions and find reality - which brings with it infinite consolation.

Violence is a non-value, it is a negativity that does not really exist and that has no effect on being. Being is made up of positivity.

Those who have sweetness and love in their hearts are moving in positivity: reality is theirs.

Blessed are those who hunger and thirst for justice, for they will be filled

Whoever desires justice and truth with all of himself, beyond concepts and ideologies, and lives for this, already participates in justice and truth, which he will never lack.

Blessed are the merciful, for they will find mercy
Blessed are the pure in heart, for they will see God
Blessed are the peaceable, for they will be called sons of God

Those who know being, also find themselves in others, they no longer have anything personal that weighs them down and binds them, and lives in a state of peace: they are already with God, and they are already one with God.

It should be noted that the "peaceable" of whom Jesus speaks are to be understood as those who have peace within themselves; translating "peaceful" with "peacemakers" is reductive and misleading.

You have heard that it was said...; but I tell you ...

The morality taught by Jesus is not based on outward fulfillments. The behaviors to adopt are rather those that arise spontaneously from knowing the truth: in those who know the truth there is no longer the slightest compromise with attitudes dictated by the illusion of being an individual separate from everything else.

Jesus' moral teaching can be summed up in his own words: "You must therefore be perfect, as your Heavenly Father is perfect", who "makes the sun rise on the wicked and the good, and makes it rain on the righteous and over the unjust". On the divine level, the categories of good and bad no longer make sense. And man's action is no different from that of God himself.

Do not accumulate treasures on earth ... instead accumulate treasures in the sky

Do not worry about what you will eat or drink ... seek first the kingdom of God and his righteousness, and all these things will be given to you in addition

Those who reside in being always have their own center in it. The practical tasks of life are then dealt with spontaneously, with ideas and actions that arise and take place from time to time.

The lamp of the body is the eye; if therefore your eye is clear, your whole body will be in the light; but if your eye is sick, your whole body will be dark

If a man knows being and resides in being, all his actions, regardless of whether or not they seem to respond to moral standards, will be perfect.

If a man, on the other hand, does not know being and does not live in being, all his actions, although it may seem that they respect moral standards, will be devoid of light and value.

Either one knows being, or one does not know it, even if those who do not know it usually delude themselves into having some understanding of being anyway.

Being on the one hand, and the illusion generated by thought on the other, belong to two levels of reality that have no bridges between them, and which are mutually exclusive.

Do not judge, so as not to be judged

Judging means looking at the world and others with the eyes of dualism. By doing this, we automatically enclose ourselves in dualism, and therefore we expose ourselves (even to our own eyes) to that same yardstick of judgement with which we are judging others.

Why do you look at the speck in your brother's eye, while you do not notice the beam that you have in your eye?

It is easy to notice the faults of others; what is not considered, however, is that there is a basic defect, which is common to all men, and in comparison to which the various defects that we encounter each other are insignificant.

The basic defect (the "beam" in our eye) consists in not being able to see the real nature, both of ourselves and of the world in which we live: a free and unlimited nature, a non-dualistic nature, not subject to time and space.

Whoever does not know God has nothing to teach others.

Ask and you will receive, seek and you will find, knock and it will be opened to you

Access to the truth is not hidden, it is not distant and inaccessible. Instead, it is always available and very handy, even in what is most common and closest to us (in Zen there is the expression "door without door").

Whatever you want men to do to you, do it to them too

This is a recommendation that presupposes the unity of the whole.

When the illusion of being separate individuals has fallen, it is natural to find others in oneself, and oneself in others.

Enter through the narrow door, because the one leading to
perdition is wide and spacious

Even though Life is spread out all around us, and we are immersed in it and are part of it, most men do not recognize it.

If you follow the common way of seeing things, you are precluded from accessing Life. Having become accustomed to gross experiences and rigid and closed thoughts, we easily overlook the subtle and delicate call of truth.

Not whoever tells me Lord, Lord, he will enter the kingdom of heaven, but he who does the will of my Father who is in heaven

He who resides in being has abandoned the illusion of being a subject, and his actions are not aimed at pursuing personal goals. He has no will of his own, because he recognizes that he does not have it and that he never had it. His actions spring spontaneously, and can therefore be defined as conforming to the will of the One (being).

There are words - those dictated by conceptual thought - whose meaning can be understood by anyone.

There are instead words that are not mental constructions, and that are spoken to awaken in the listener an understanding that the mind cannot conceive. Such words are like the finger pointing to the moon.

Only those who have the ability to go beyond the dualistic mind will be able to see the moon indicated by the finger. Others will believe they have listened, but they will actually only see the finger, because they will not know how to go beyond the conceptual sphere of words.

As for the resurrection of the dead, it is written: I am the God of Abraham, and the God of Isaac, and the God of Jacob. He is the God of the living, not the dead!

Imagining that, at the end of time, there is a resurrection of the dead, means conceiving a chronological succession of events, thus applying the concept of time to a dimension that is foreign to it.

Imagining a before and after is the mode of the conceptual mind. On the other hand, God is eternity, that is, the absence of time.

In the world of appearances, everything is born and dies. In the reality of being, no one is born and no one dies, but everything is alive in God.

There is nothing secret that is not made known, and nothing hidden that is not brought to light

Secret things and hidden things can only exist in the world of appearance. In the reality of being, everything is simultaneous, manifest and in full light.

Whoever does not welcome the kingdom of God as a child will not enter it

Spontaneity, innocence, humility, receptivity, the absence of an ego: these are the characteristics of those who know how to open themselves to the knowledge of being.

True goodness presupposes the total absence of any personal reference. Anyone who thinks he is a separate individual cannot be considered good.

Referring to oneself as a subject corrupts and disqualifies every action and every thought, however altruistic they may seem.

Goodness is only possible in the absence of duality, therefore only in the One, in God.

Someone can be good, therefore, only if he has overcome the ignorance of duality, and recognizes himself in the One.

It is easier for a camel to pass through the eye of a needle, that a rich man enters the kingdom of God

The basis of "wealth" lies in the belief that one has individuality. Without an I there is no possession.

Anyone who was deprived of any material good, but was still a victim of the illusion of being an ego, would already be too "rich" to enter the realm of being.

If your eye scandalizes you, tear it out: it is better for you to enter the kingdom of God with one eye than to be cast with two eyes into Gehenna

What belongs to the dimension of appearance has no real value; the only thing that really matters is the act of reconnecting to our true nature, to being.

Even the apparently most burdensome sacrifice is infinitely negligible when compared to the good of abiding in being.

Whoever exalts himself will be humbled, and whoever humbles himself will be exalted

In the reality of being, laws diametrically opposed to those of the world of appearance are in force. While in the world of appearance one wins by strengthening the structure of the ego, in the reality of being the one who no longer gives weight to the ego wins.

As for that day and hour, however, no one knows, not even the angels of heaven and not even the Son of man, but only the Father ... Watch therefore, because you do not know on which day your Lord will come

There is no time in being. It is therefore not possible to plan or predict the encounter with the being. This meeting can only take place in the presence of a willingness to touch reality without mediations and expectations.

What I am saying to you, I am saying to everyone: watch!

The exhortation to be awake is not just a warning to be immediately available for the encounter with being. It also alludes to the task of getting out of the sleep state in which man lives.

Man is currently trapped in his mental representations of the world: from this dream condition he is called to awaken, to see reality directly.

Any sin will be forgiven, but the blasphemy against the Spirit will not be forgiven

We are not "our" body, we are not "our" personality, we are not "our" soul or "our" spirit. What we are cannot be described or imagined, so immense is it.

Therefore our every action, even the most stupid or the most atrocious, is not really "ours", and can easily be "forgiven" and overcome when we recognize our true nature, that is, when we recognize ourselves in being.

However, if we "sin against the Spirit", that is, if we deny our true nature by refusing to open ourselves to it, no forgiveness will be possible. And the condemnation will be to continue to remain prisoners of illusion.

Who is without sin cast the first stone

Whenever you feel compelled to judge and condemn someone else, it may be convenient to stop first and reflect on this: are we ourselves free from the "sin" that underlies all others, that is, identification with the self?

Unless one is born again from on high, he cannot see the kingdom
of God

The birth of the physical body is not the true birth. Only when one knows one's being and discovers one's true nature does true creation take place, and one really enters life.

If the rebirth in being does not take place, existence remains only a pale dream, evanescent and devoid of value.

The wind blows where it wants, you don't know where it comes from and where it goes. So it is with anyone who is born of the Spirit

The one who is reborn in the Being, and dwells in it, no longer identifies himself with a physical body, with a personal history and with certain psychological characteristics. Others may still see him this way, but in reality he lives in total freedom, without borders and without a goal.

The Son can do nothing by himself, if not what he sees the Father doing

My judgment is right, because I am not looking for my will, but for the will of the One who sent me

When the deceptive identification with an individual conscience has been overcome, one's actions and judgments are no longer conditioned by what we considered "our" history and by what we felt as "our" needs.

Quite simply, now thoughts arise in the mind, and actions occur spontaneously.

They are actions and thoughts that are no longer just "ours", but of the whole universe.

If you don't believe that I Am, you will die in your sins

Before Abraham was, I Am

The name of God is I Am.

The being, the I Am, is out of time.

Time is a modality in which being apparently manifests itself, but being precedes time, just as what is real precedes what is apparent.

Whoever knows being knows God, knows himself, and is free from illusion.

"Sin" means conforming one's life to individual criteria, rather than to the mind of God. And this is the inevitable horizon of those who do not recognize that individual identity is illusory.

If anyone keeps my word, he will never see death

Both birth and death exist only in the dimension of appearance, in which the mind creates the differences and the illusion of temporal succession.

Those who know and live the truth no longer undergo reductive mental representations.

Opening up to being involves overcoming the belief in birth and death.

He who eats my flesh and drinks my blood has eternal life ... he
abides in me, and I in him

Being is the source of everything, and being is everything.

Being is in everything, and everything is in being.

Whatever part of the mineral, vegetable or animal world we use or sacrifice to keep us alive, we are using and sacrificing being.

It is the very being that lives and suffers in everything we sacrifice on our path.

But it is also being itself that offers itself in sacrifice for us, because the nature of being is precisely to give oneself, to sacrifice oneself for love.

If we abide in being, we understand and participate in this sacrifice of love.

The kingdom of God does not come in such a way as to be noticed, and it cannot be said: here it is, or there it is. For behold, the kingdom of God is among you!

If one searches among what belongs to the world of appearance, one will never find being, but always only different aspects of that same dualistic and illusory world.

When we stop looking, we realize that being is already here, and that it always has been.

This is the overturning of the ego logic. And this reversal is the characteristic of those who dwell in being.

In fact, being does not make any distinctions, it leaves nothing and no one out. Being is always totally available to everyone, without preferences, without calculations.

Being is only positive: it is giving, pouring out, creating, loving.

You will know the truth, and the truth will make you free

Knowing the truth means getting out of the deception of the mind, which encloses us in a dualistic world.

By recognizing ourselves as part of being and equal to being, all apparent limitations and apparent chains fall away, and we discover that freedom that is ours by birthright.

Only those who know being and abide in being can understand and follow the words of those who express being.

For others, such words will only be new concepts. They will discuss and construct other concepts on them, thus moving further and further away from the possibility of understanding them.

Is it not written: "I said: you are gods"?

In being there are no distinctions or limits. Being is everything, and everything is in being.

Anyone who recognizes being and recognizes himself in being, knows that he cannot exist without being, and that being could not exist without him.

No matter how minimal and insignificant it may seem in the eyes of the world: in every smallest part of the universe there is God, in all his immensity.

To say that every man is God is the pure truth. And it remains true, even for those in whom that awareness has not yet matured.

I speak to them in parables, because it is given to you to know the mysteries of the kingdom of heaven, but to them it is not given

Jesus justifies the use of parables by quoting Isaiah ("They will see without seeing, they will listen without understanding"). It is inevitable that some are destined to understand the truth, and some are not. It's not about merit and guilt, it's just a fact.

Parables are a means of helping those who are unable to see the truth directly. Thanks to them, the normal way of understanding reality is overturned, and common schemes are blown up.

Reliving within ourselves the scenes illustrated by the parables, a resonance can occur that allows us to intuit that truth that has always been in front of us.

Clarified Version of the Prayer of the Our Father

Commonly adopted version:

Our Father in heaven,
hallowed be your name,
your kingdom come,
your will be done, on earth as it is in heaven,
give us this day our daily bread,
and forgive us our debts,
as we also have forgiven our debtors,
and do not bring us to the time of trial,
but rescue us from evil.

Clarified version:

Source of all being,
who reside in eternity,
may your domain be revealed
according to your will, as well as in time as out of time,
feed our life now,
undo the wrongs we've done,
as we undo the wrongs we have suffered,
and do not lead us to a defective life,
but free us from every mistake.

Notes to the clarified version of the Our Father

Each prayer, in its profound meaning, should not be understood as a request aimed at obtaining help in the future. It is rather a description of a reality. True prayer is always, so to speak, immediately answered.

God is "Father" because he is the being, that is, our true essence.

The "heavens" are not a separate and higher world than the earthly world: they are the ultimate reality, out of time, of which this same world is a manifestation.

The next three sentences of the prayer are the statement that being is everything, and there are no powers or wills that are external to it.

If we reside in being, we receive life in abundance at every instant, and having dissolved the deception of believing ourselves to be separate and limited individuals, we are free from holding ourselves and others responsible for the mistakes that have been made.

Some argue that God cannot want to "lead us into temptation"; but in this way the absolute power of him is denied: nothing can happen, if not by the "will" of being. In reality, the last sentences of the prayer are a self-exhortation not to come out of being, that is, not to fall into the illusion of an individual existence.

Printed in Great Britain
by Amazon

45833186R00076